Professor Longhair
COLLECTION

Transcriptions by Josh Paxton

Cover Photo: Michael P. Smith

ISBN 978-0-7935-9334-7

HAL•LEONARD®
CORPORATION
7777 W. BLUEMOUND RD. P.O. BOX 13819 MILWAUKEE, WI 53213

Visit Hal Leonard Online at
www.halleonard.com

Professor Longhair
COLLECTION

Contents

Biography		4
Discography		128

SONG	ALBUM TITLE	PAGE #
BALDHEAD	CRAWFISH FIESTA	6
BIG CHIEF	Composite transcription from CRAWFISH FIESTA and FESS' GUMBO	10
CRAWFISH FIESTA	CRAWFISH FIESTA	19
DOIN' IT	FESS' GUMBO	46
GONE SO LONG	HOUSEPARTY NEW ORLEANS STYLE	26
GONNA LEAVE THIS TOWN	HOUSEPARTY NEW ORLEANS STYLE	34
HEY LITTLE GIRL	NEW ORLEANS PIANO	40
HEY NOW BABY	Composite transcription from THE COMPLETE LONDON CONCERT, FESS' GUMBO and NEW ORLEANS PIANO	53
HOW LONG HAS THAT TRAIN BEEN GONE	ROCK 'N ROLL GUMBO	80
JUNCO PARTNER	ROCK 'N ROLL GUMBO	60
MARDI GRAS IN NEW ORLEANS	Composite transcription from THE COMPLETE LONDON CONCERT, NEW ORLEANS PIANO and ROCK 'N ROLL GUMBO	68
MEAN OL' WORLD	ROCK 'N ROLL GUMBO	74
MEET ME TOMORROW NIGHT	ROCK 'N ROLL GUMBO	85
MESS AROUND	Composite transcription from FESS' GUMBO and ROCK 'N ROLL GUMBO	92
NO BUTS NO MAYBES	HOUSEPARTY NEW ORLEANS STYLE	99
SHE WALKS RIGHT IN	HOUSEPARTY NEW ORLEANS STYLE	112
STAG-O-LEE	ROCK 'N ROLL GUMBO	104
THANK YOU PRETTY BABY	HOUSEPARTY NEW ORLEANS STYLE	117
TIPITINA	Composite transcription from FESS' GUMBO and ROCK 'N ROLL GUMBO	122

Biography

Known as the Godfather of New Orleans piano, Professor Longhair was born Henry Roeland Byrd on December 19, 1918 in Bogalusa, Louisiana. His family moved to New Orleans shortly afterward. Byrd received some musical instruction from his mother, although he would later say that his first instruments were the bottoms of his feet; he tap-danced for change on the streets of the French Quarter as a child.

Byrd didn't develop a serious interest in music until his late teens. He was performing with a dance troupe, and had to fill in for the group's drummer one night. Tuts Washington, pianist with the group, encouraged Byrd to continue with the drums, which he did. However, he soon grew tired of carrying the drum set around and switched to piano instead. Tuts was one of his early mentors. Byrd also received encouragement from barrelhouse pianist Sullivan Rock, who showed him how to play "Pinetop's Boogie Woogie."

One of the strongest influences on his style came from a job he took with a government road crew. The job involved travel, and during his six-month tenure, he was exposed to a variety of Latin and Caribbean bands. Drawn to the rhythmic elements of the music, he incorporated them into his playing. Blended with the blues and barrelhouse styles, his unique piano style would have an immeasurable impact on New Orleans music.

Byrd went into the army in 1942, and after a medical discharge two years later, spent several years as a cook and a professional card player (throughout his life, gambling was always his 'second profession'). Although he played occasional piano jobs, he wasn't noticed as a musician until 1948, when during another band's break, he played a few songs at a club. His performance created such a stir that the club owner fired the band and hired Byrd. It was during this stint that he got the name Professor Longhair, due to the ponytail he sported at the time. His accompanying band was known as the Three Hair Combo (Professor Longhair, Professor Shorthair and Professor No Hair).

A recording boom was taking place in New Orleans, and Byrd jumped on it in 1949, recording four songs for a small label. Because the session didn't meet union regulations, the sides weren't released. But Byrd was approached by other labels. By the end of 1950 he recorded what would be two of his most famous songs: "Baldhead," which made it to the #5 position on the R&B charts, and "Mardi Gras in New Orleans," which remains one of the perennially popular songs in the Crescent City.

Byrd continued to record during the early '50s and one of these would become his signature piece, "Tipitina." However, his success outside of New Orleans was limited, partially because he frequently changed labels and monikers. He was billed as either Professor Longhair, Roy Byrd, Roeland Byrd or Robert Byrd. His band was called such diverse names as the Blues Scholars, the Blues Jumpers, and the Shuffling Hungarians(!) But in New Orleans, everyone knew who he was, and most people simply called him 'Fess.'

Fess had a stroke in 1954, leaving him unable to play for a time. In 1955 he managed to play on a few sessions as a sideman, but did not record as a leader again until 1957. His singles included the locally popular "No Buts No Maybes." He soon faded from the public eye, playing occasional gigs and making no new recordings for several years.

In 1964, he returned to the studio to record "Big Chief," penned by local songwriting legend Earl King. The song featured an all-star band (including his one-time student, Mac Rebennack, on guitar), a stunning horn arrangement, and one of Fess' most unique and memorable piano licks. Although the record did not sell as successfully as it should have, it would eventually become a New Orleans anthem. Despite its lack of commercial success, Fess' spirits were buoyed, and he slowly started playing around town in local clubs and private parties.

He probably would have lived out the rest of his days in that manner if not for Quint Davis and Allison Minor Kaslow, two young New Orleans music aficionados who were instrumental in launching the New Orleans Jazz and Heritage Festival in the early '70s. They knew of Fess only through recordings, but were determined to find him and include him in the festival. It took them a year to track him down, and the man they found was in sad shape, sweeping the floor at a local record store. He was living in poverty, couldn't eat, and could barely walk. But when he managed to take the stage for the 1971 Festival, his life and career took a major turn. He gave an exhilarating performance that literally brought the rest of the festival to a halt. Festival musicians and audience members witnessed the return of Professor Longhair.

With Davis as his manager, Fess set about rebuilding his career. He played in local clubs again, and a demo tape got him a European tour with the Meters. Although he made several new recordings, none of them were released until much later; the only 'new' Professor Longhair album was a compilation of his Atlantic singles from 1949 and 1953. Since the original discs had become prized collector's items, the album did well and boosted Fess' career even further.

Tragedy struck in 1974, when the house that served as his family home and rehearsal space was destroyed in a fire. No one was hurt, but the house was uninsured and everything Fess had was lost. He was left with nothing. But the local music community came to his aid with benefit concerts, and ironically, a recording session arranged to help him out yielded what is widely regarded as his best album of the mid-'70s, *Rock 'n Roll Gumbo*.

Fess gained further attention in 1976 when Paul McCartney asked him to play a private party on the Queen Mary riverboat. Although Fess didn't know who McCartney was (!), he gladly took the job and his performance was recorded and released as his next album. He got another break in 1977 when a venue formerly known as the 501 Club reopened under the name Tipitina's, for the specific purpose of giving him a regular place to play. By 1978 he was living comfortably from his music for the first time in his life.

In 1979 Fess participated, along with Allen Toussaint and Tuts Washington, in the video documentary "Piano Players Rarely Ever Play Together," and also signed a contract with Chicago's Alligator Records. For the album, he was supported by a crack team of New Orleans musicians, including his one-time student Mac Rebennack making a rare appearance on guitar. *Crawfish Fiesta* is among the best recordings of his career, and those who knew Fess say he was prouder of it than of anything else he had recorded. It went on to win the W.C. Handy award for Best Blues Album of the Year. It's especially sad, then, that he did not live to see its release; on January 30, 1980, the night before the album was released, Professor Longhair died of a heart attack in his home. His funeral was one of the most widely attended of any New Orleans musician.

Longhair's importance in the history of New Orleans music can hardly be overemphasized. Virtually every New Orleans pianist to come after him has openly acknowledged his as a powerful influence. In fact, the vast majority of New Orleans R&B and funk bands have claimed Fess as an influence. Although he is sometimes accused of having been a 'sloppy' piano player, the music presented in this collection should dispel any misconceptions of technical inadequacy on his part; what he lacked in pianistic virtuosity, he more than made up in rhythmic sophistication and originality. His songs have been recorded by musicians too numerous to mention, and are still played regularly by Dr. John, the Meters, and the Neville Brothers. What is often overlooked is his impact on popular music outside of New Orleans. His vocal style influenced Elvis Presley to such an extent that many contemporary listeners, upon hearing Fess for the first time, comment on how much he 'sounds like Elvis.' In fact, it was Elvis who sounded like Fess. Furthermore, the roots of funk and its various offshoots can be traced back to rhythmic innovations evident in Fess' music as early as 1949. The drum part on the original recording of "Big Chief" (played by Smokey Johnson) is frequently described as sounding 'like a James Brown groove,' although at the time "Big Chief" was recorded, Brown's music had not approached that level of syncopation. It's also fair to say that his influence can be heard in many American pop songs of the last forty years.

But perhaps the place where his influence is still most strongly felt is at the club named after his best-loved song. It is located at the corner of Napoleon and Tchoupitoulas in New Orleans. The club also has his likeness on a huge banner, a life-sized statue, and a head-and-shoulders bust, (which patrons and musicians alike are encouraged to rub for good luck). There at Tipitina's, the city's piano players all gather once a year during Piano Night. Throughout the course of the evening, players ranging from seasoned pros to young upstarts pay homage to the music of Professor Longhair. Despite the changes in musical evolution in the last fifty years, Fess' music remains as vital today as it ever was.

Josh Paxton

BALDHEAD

By Henry Roeland Byrd

there, *(Bald* *head)* she ain't got _____ no _____

hair. _____

BIG CHIEF

By Earl King

12

Me ___ got a fire me can't put out.
tribe. ___

Me ___ fire wa - ter gon - na make me ___ shout.
Got ___ my squaw right by my side. ___

Me __ big chief; I'm feel - in' good. __
We __ gon' dance til the mor - ning come. __

Uh, me big chief; I got a

(Whistle 8va)

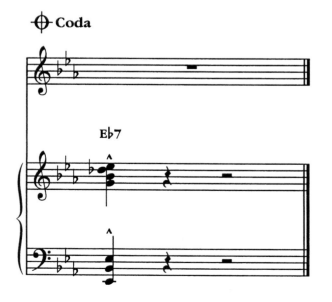

CRAWFISH FIESTA

By Henry Roeland Byrd

GONE SO LONG

By Henry Roeland Byrd

Medium Blues

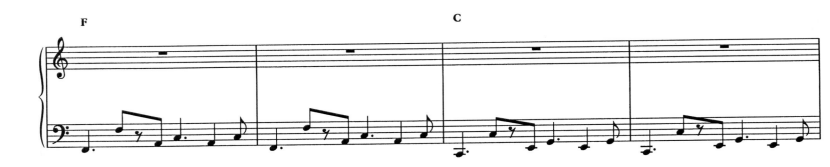

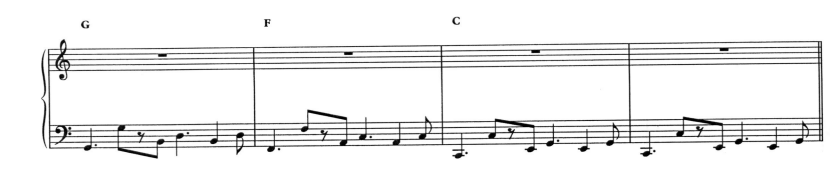

GONNA LEAVE THIS TOWN

By Henry Roeland Byrd

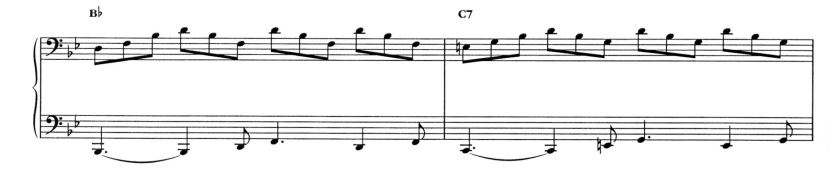

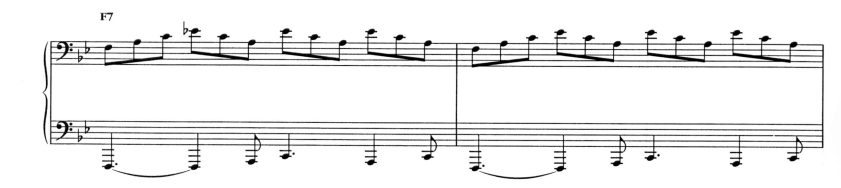

36

HEY LITTLE GIRL

By Henry Roeland Byrd

Left hand 8vb throughout

(Spoken) Hey now, who's that fine little girl over there by the

door, man? She sure looks fine to me. What's her name? Look out,

let me call her one time.

43

Hey lit-tle girl, _____ thank _ you for ev-'ry-thing. _____ Hey _____

_ lit-tle girl, _ thank you for ev-'ry-thing. _____ Well I know

now I'm in love _ with you, _ hope you _ feel the same. _____

DOIN' IT

By Henry Roeland Byrd

49

50

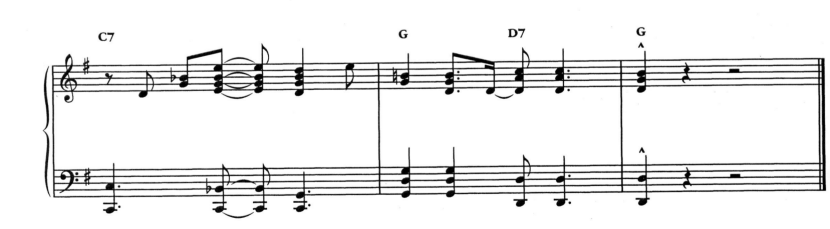

HEY NOW BABY

By Henry Roeland Byrd

F7

C

G7

C

G7

C

Hey ___ now ba - by,

hey ___ now hon - ey child.

JUNCO PARTNER

By Robert Ellen and Mack Ellen

Lyric: Oh   down   the   road

MARDI GRAS IN NEW ORLEANS

By Henry Roeland Byrd

72

MEAN OL' WORLD

Arranged by Henry Roeland Byrd

Medium Blues

♩. = 92

Yes, ___ it's a mean _____ ol' ___ world ___

HOW LONG HAS THAT
TRAIN BEEN GONE

By Henry Roeland Byrd

no real good lov - in' since my ba - by got on _____ board.

Well, how long_

MEET ME TOMORROW NIGHT

By Henry Roeland Byrd

Fast Rhumba
♩ = 194

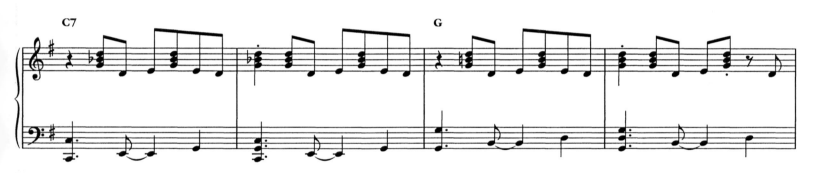

Hey ba-

MESS AROUND

**Words and Music by
Ahmet Ertegun**

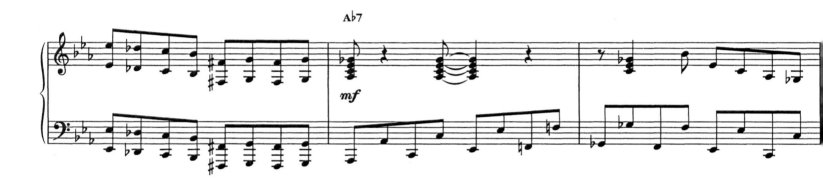

Ev - 'ry - bod - y Charles _ messed a - round. _

NO BUTS NO MAYBES

By Henry Roeland Byrd

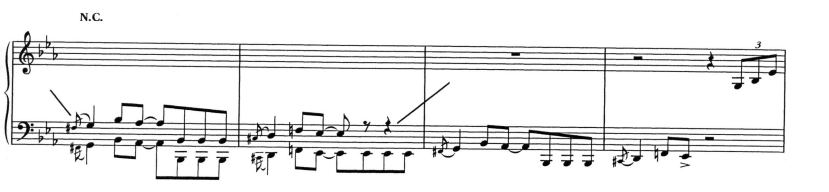

Ba - by, _____ no buts _____ and no may - bes.

Dar - ling you're driv - ing me cra - zy, I did - n't do noth - in' to you. _____

STAG-O-LEE

Arranged by Henry Roeland Byrd

Rock Rhumba

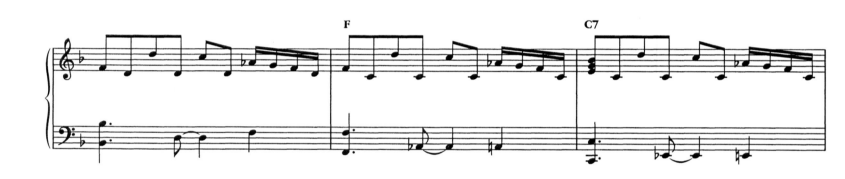

It was ear - ly, ear - ly one mor -

Bil - ly, "Yes, I _____ know you got a cute boy and girl. But if you

wan - na see your fam - 'ly, Bil - ly, meet 'em in an - oth - er world." ___

SHE WALKS RIGHT IN

By Henry Roeland Byrd

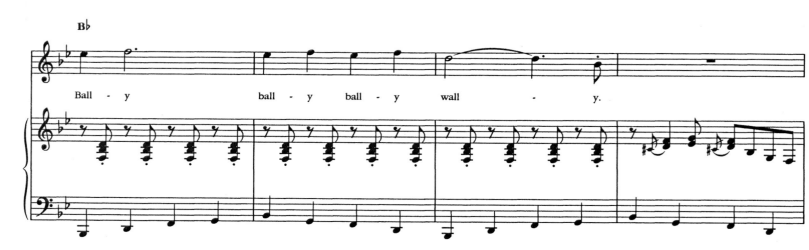

Ball - y ball - y ball - y wall - y.

116

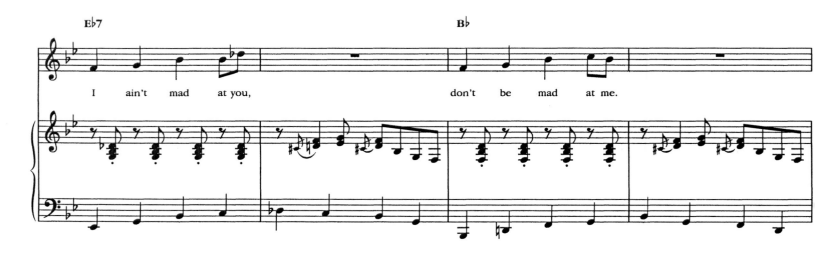

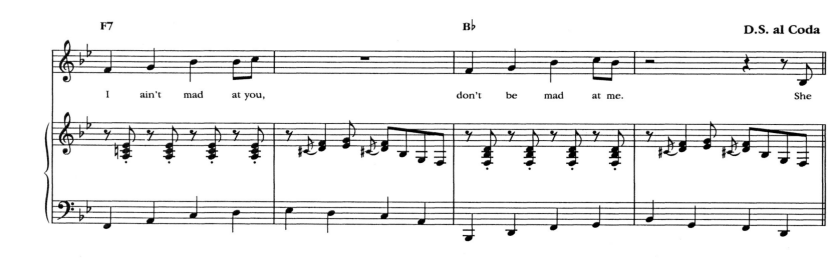

THANK YOU PRETTY BABY

By Henry Roeland Byrd

TIPITINA

By Henry Roeland Byrd

123

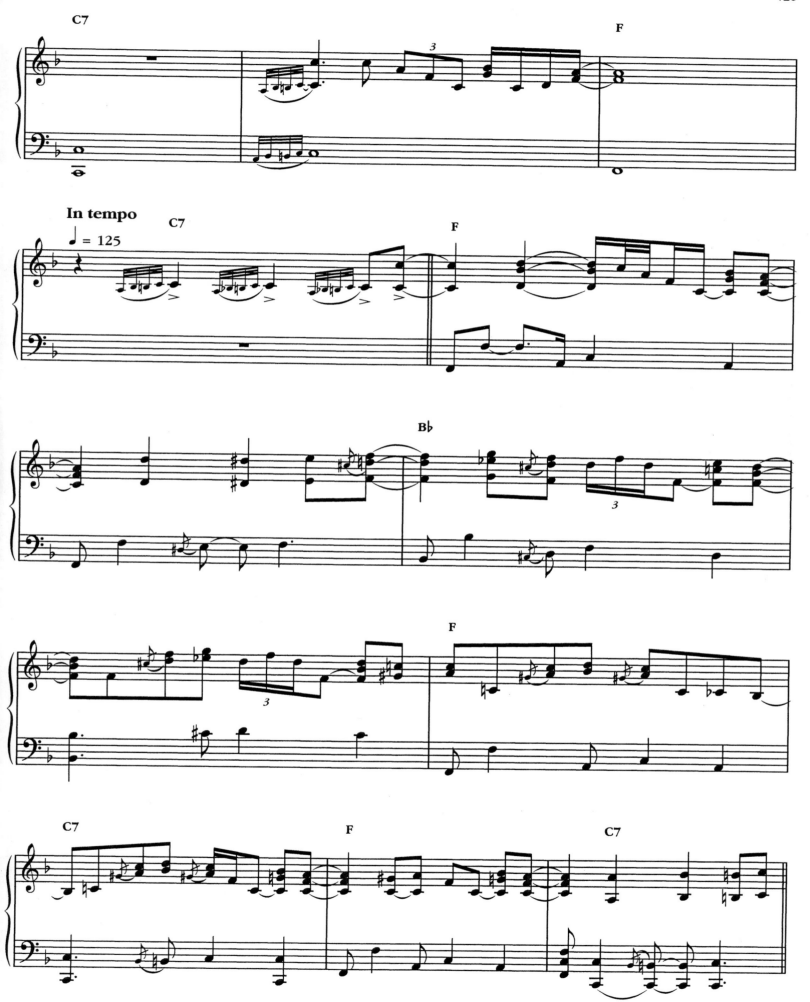

1. Tra — la - la - la - la,　　　　　　　　　　　tra - la — la - la - lay,

2, 3, 4, 5, 6 - *See additional lyrics*

tra - la - la - la　　　tra - la　na - na - nay. —

Last Time To Coda

Additional lyrics

2:
Tipitina, tra-la-la-la,
Woa lal-a tra-la-la,
Tipitina mall-a wall-a dall-a
Tra-la tee-nee-na.

3:
Hey Loberta, oh Loberta,
Girl, you hear me callin' you.
Well, you are three times seven baby,
And you know what you want to do.

4:
Hey Loberta, oh Loberta,
Girl, you tell me where you been.
When you come home this mornin', honey,
You had your belly full of gin.

5:
Tra-la-la tee-nee-na-na,
Tipitina tra-la-la,
Tipitina oo-la mall-a wall-a dall-a
Tra-la tee-na-na.

6:
Come on boy, we're goin' down on the corner,
Well, we sure gonna have ourselves a good time.
We're gonna tipi-trall-a mall-a wall-a;
Drink that mill-a mill-a wine.

Discography

THE COMPLETE LONDON CONCERT	JSP CD 202
CRAWFISH FIESTA	ALLIGATOR ALCD 4718
FESS' GUMBO	STONY PLAIN SPCD 1214
HOUSEPARTY NEW ORLEANS STYLE	ROUNDER CD 2057
NEW ORLEANS PIANO	ATLANTIC JAZZ 7225
ROCK 'N ROLL GUMBO	DANCING CAT DD 3006